D1262724

Beginning Nonviolence

Learning and Teaching Nonviolence
To Use Every Day

by

John Looney and Kezia Sproat

Highbank Farm Peace Education Center
Chillicothe, Ohio

published by

Skye's The Limit Publishing & Public Relations, LLC
U.S.A.

Beginning Nonviolence – Learning and Teaching Nonviolence To Use Every Day
© 2013 by Kezia Sproat. All rights reserved.

Published by *Skye's The Limit Publishing & Public Relations, LLC*

This book may not be reproduced in whole or in part, in any form or by any means, electronic or mechanical, including photocopying, recording, or by any information storage and retrieval system now known or hereafter invented, without written permission from the publisher and/or author.

Books published by Skye's The Limit Publishing & Public Relations, LLC may be available at special discounts for bulk purchases in the United States by corporations, institutions, and other organizations. For more information, please contact the Marketing Department at Skye's The Limit Publishing & Public Relations, P.O. Box 133, Galena, Ohio 43021, (fax) 740-548-4929; or via e-mail at talk2stl@gmail.com

Book design and cover copyright ©2013 by Skye's The Limit Publishing & Public Relations, LLC. All Rights Reserved.

Cover, design, and typography by Cheryl A. Johnson

Cover photo by K. Hurley, ©2010 - Creative Commons License
http://www.flickr.com/photos/18886807@N00/4885294279/

Skye's the Limit Publishing & Public Relations
PO Box 133, Galena, Ohio 43021
(fax) 740-548-4929
skyesthelimitpublishing.blogspot.com

Published in the United States of America. Second Printing.

Paperback:

ISBN-13: 978-1-939044-10-5
ISBN-10: 1939044103

Kindle eBook (available January 2014):
ISBN-13: 978-1-939044-11-2
ISBN-10: 1939044111

Website: BeginningNonviolence.blogspot.com

Library of Congress Control Number: 2013955226

PUBLISHER'S NOTE

Every possible effort has been made to ensure that the information contained in this book is accurate at the time of going to press, and the publisher and author cannot accept responsibility for any errors and omissions, however caused. No responsibility for loss or damage occasioned by any person acting, or refraining from action, as a result of the material in this publication can be accepted by the editor, the publisher, or the author.

1

Differences Between
Violence and Nonviolence

Adapted from the *Alternatives to Violence Workbook*, Akron, OH: Peace Grows, Inc.,
©1985

VIOLENCE	NONVIOLENCE
Goal	
To defeat the opponent to a finish. Must humiliate, injure, corner, or destroy the opponent. Win while the opponent loses.	To make friends with and then work with the opponent. To understand and change attitudes in order to solve the problem together. To reach a mutually satisfactory settlement where both sides win.
Attitude	
Requires a strong hatred and fear of the opponent to stimulate the necessary rage to attack and harm.	Requires a friendly and caring attitude toward the opponent. Carefully avoid any sort of harm to the opponent in order to overcome their hatred and fear. Aim toward a mutually beneficial agreement. Summon courage to think and act clearly, and self-control for holding firmly to one's goals and values even while suffering an attack.

VIOLENCE	NONVIOLENCE
Principles and Techniques	
1. Attack so strongly that the opponent seems to have no alternatives or choices.	1. Keep many options open for the opponent to change their position and move toward resolving the conflict as easily as possible and without losing face. One technique is to set up a dilemma for the opponent so that any choice leads to a solution.
2. Inflict all possible suffering on the opponent.	2. Completely reject all use of any form of violence.
3. Avoid one's own suffering at all costs.	3. Be willing to suffer oneself but completely unwilling to cause suffering to someone else. The utmost courage is required.
4. Use all resources to get victory as soon as possible.	4. Be persistent and patient in reaching an equitable solution that is acceptable to all parties. Realize that equitable, lasting change comes slowly.

VIOLENCE	NONVIOLENCE
5. Use any means to attain victory.	5. Remain thoroughly dedicated to justice throughout the entire process.
6. Manipulate public opinion to distort the truth where it serves your purposes, or to cover your own wrongful conduct.	6. Remain constantly faithful to the truth at all times and at all costs. Maintain conduct and public relations as exemplary and truthful as possible to prompt sympathy and understanding in the opponent and the public.
7. Complete rigid training in the use of arms and techniques to destroy the opponent under firm discipline.	7. Complete rigid training in all nonviolent principles, techniques, skills, and discipline to carry out the nonviolent strategy.
8. Act arrogantly to instill hatred and fear.	8. Act with integrity and humility, which instill respect and sympathy.
9. Be harmful.	9. Be helpful.

VIOLENCE	NONVIOLENCE
10. Rely mostly on physical resources.	10. Rely mostly on mental, creative and moral resources.
11. Stimulate hatred toward the opponent.	11. Show respect and caring for the opponent. "Love your enemy" is a valid, necessary nonviolent principle.
12. Ignore or suppress a problem which does violence to others, if possible.	12. Expose all facts so the public, the opponent and allies have full understanding and knowledge on which to base decisions and acts.
13. Use all possible concerted negative words and actions against the opponent.	13. All words and actions emphasize the positive for change and reconciliation, even where it is difficult and risky.
14. All violent actions become predictable – aimed at the opponent's destruction and the established norms for fighting.	14. Actions often are unexpected and unpredictable because they do not follow the normal cultural pattern. The element of surprise aids nonviolent success.

2 The Nature of Violence

Our culture is extremely violent. The last 100 years recorded more devastating wars than in the total of human history. Technology has progressed, but ethics hasn't. What can we do to reduce violence? We can begin by focusing on what it is and how it grows. Because shootings, stabbings, rapes, bombings and wars get top billing in the media—they drive up ratings and advertising sales—such crimes easily can be taken to define what we mean by the word "violence." Most mass media news coverage tends to reinforce the idea that physical might, force, and strength can get a person what they want, that physical force solves problems. Many of us have allowed the media to define what is "real."

Nonviolent solutions to problems aren't often "news," so they're not often reported. The idea thus develops that either that there is no such thing as effective nonviolence, or, if there is, then it doesn't work in the "real" world.

Certainly beatings and murders hurt victims. But all hurts aren't physical. Name-calling, exclusion, ridicule, "put-downs" like eye-rolling, discrimination, disrespect, threats, poverty, and racism are also violent. Even interrupting when someone else is talking is a form of violence. **To understand violence, we must expand our concept of what it is.** If we list all the actions, or inactions, that hurt people, we come to a much broader definition of violence.

In *Alternatives to Violence* classes, we ask participants, working as a group, to list examples of violence, naming every type they can think of. If necessary, we prompt to include snubbing, interrupting, giving someone the "silent treatment," dumping trash in the wrong place, fraudulent financial dealings, etc. Next we study the list to find what all the examples have in common, and try to agree on the answer, using consensus.

The common thread that runs through all the offered examples of violence is that **something is being hurt**: If we understand and define violence as whatever hurts life–not just the sensational bombings, murders and rapes–we can begin to find new ways to deal with it. Using this very broad definition, we see violence in our own actions. Instead of saying "I'm certainly not violent! I'm not beating or killing anyone!" we can begin to understand that we too may behave violently. Therefore, studying and understanding violence and how to reduce and prevent it, can help all of us in handling our own lives. Recognizing small examples can also help us understand and deal with the huge scope of violence in our culture.

3 Differentiate Conflict, Anger, and Violence.

Although many people use the words "conflict" and "violence" interchangeably, they are not synonyms. Conflict is necessary for growth: the soil must give way for the daffodil. Teenagers must find their own identities. To live in complex societies, citizens must pay taxes and obey restrictive laws, based on the common good.

It is very helpful to memorize these definitions:

- **Conflict is a good and normal part of life, necessary for growth.**

- **Anger is a normal, common, useful human emotion. It is OK. Anger can give us energy needed to bring about change.**

- **Violence is a common but useless response to conflict and anger.**

Conflict is often felt internally: Should I go to the movies or do the laundry? Divorce my spouse? Quit my job? Buy a new car that's under warranty or a used car with a great track record? Rent an apartment or buy a house? Get supper from the deli or cook at home? Allow the teenager to use the car or not? Those are all conflicts, or choices, that we solve, and in so doing, build or hinder our own lives.

Anger can be internal as well: we get angry at ourselves for making silly mistakes and for not doing what we know to

be most efficient: Why didn't I pay taxes on time and avoid the penalty? Why didn't I remember the stop signs had been removed from oncoming traffic and avoid that crash? Angry feelings can give us energy and willpower to avoid repeating our errors. Anger gives me energy to write this book: I am angry that stereotyping can still lead to murder in my native country.

Stereotypes and how they work.

Marsha Hamilton,[3] a librarian at The Ohio State University, has written the clearest definition of 'stereotype' I've ever seen.

> A stereotype is an image, trait, or mode of behavior that is inappropriately applied to all individuals who share a common religion, sex, ethnic origin, geographic location, political party, socio-economic bracket, or other discernible factor that may set them apart from others. One hallmark of a stereotype is its persistence over time. An event or character can enter popular awareness, and through retelling and exaggeration, transform into an image that comes to represent millions of individuals for dozens or hundreds of years.
>
> Stereotypes have a specific effect on the way the holder processes incoming information. The holder of a stereotype will accept any information, no matter how improbable, which reinforces the image. Conversely, the holder will discard as irrelevant any data which does not confirm the stereotype.

---

3   Hamilton, Marsha J., The Arab Woman in U.S. Popular Culture: Sex and Stereotype. *Food for Our Grandmothers: Writings by Arab-American and Arab-Canadian Feminists*, Ed. Joanna Kadi, Boston: South End Press, 1994, pp. 173-174.

A stereotype is a shortcut. It allows novelists, artists, cartoonists, news reporters, and politicians to raise an image and make a point without having to provide tedious background information. "Right-wing Christian" or "left-wing Muslim" can define a complex coalition of people in an unknown part of the world in a short phrase. The viewer understands exactly how he or she is supposed to feel about each group. Announcers guide our reactions to an event such as a bombing by making the object either a "refugee camp" or a "guerrilla base." While one term may elicit an expression of concern or outrage, the other does not. Stereotypes allow the holder to easily identify one group as "us" and another as "them." This can produce a reassuring sense of self-identification. A stereotype gives the holder the ability to easily judge who is right and wrong in complex situations. It instills a feeling of cultural superiority over beings unlike oneself.

Violence can be against ourselves, as we know: addiction, suicide, self-deprecating comments. Small acts of violence, e.g., interrupting, smirking, etc., hurt other people and often prompt escalation, the need to "get back at" whoever has "hurt" us. In studying nonviolence, we learn to look at others who would "hurt" us in a new way. As Jesus of Nazareth advised, we can turn the other cheek, return love for hate, and *in so doing we become more powerful.*

The Salt March led by Gandhi in India electrified the world in 1930 because protesters submitted to violence without fighting back. In the 1960s the Civil Rights Movement in the United States was successful because Dr. King, who studied

Gandhi, and many others had learned that power comes from nonviolence. They changed the culture of the United States in one generation. Other historical examples abound, of power that grows monumentally through nonviolence.

This book focuses on nonviolence that can be used by individuals every day, so that their lives are happier. Small examples can be overlooked: in early 2012, in Florida, Natalie Jackson, an attorney for Trayvon Martin's family, for example, showed her knowledge of nonviolence when she responded to an interviewer goading her for a response to Martin's killer's father, who had accused President Obama of expressing hatred (The president had said, "If I had a son, he would look like Trayvon.") Instead of lambasting the old man, Ms. Jackson replied, "I understand. He is a father, trying to protect his son." The interviewer was looking for outrage, but Ms. Jackson's nonviolent, kind answer helped defuse a small part of the tragedy. She also saved her own energy.

Conflict is everywhere, in every workplace, every church, every normal home. Think of a willful toddler who refuses to wear her shoes when the family is ready to leave the house in the morning. Conflict is what the family experiences. The family must leave the house together, but the toddler wants to go barefoot, which is not okay with the parents. The parents may feel anger at the toddler and vice versa. The parents may take their anger even further and characterize the child in a negative way verbally; that is, call the child a name. Name calling, hitting, or spanking the child is violence. It's extremely easy for parents to let their anger turn to violence. However, doing so only creates more problems for the parents (and the children) as the children grow.

When a parent acknowledges their own anger before they become violent, they can learn ways to release their anger nonviolently. Sometimes just owning up to their anger is all it takes to defuse the conflict, "Oh! I feel so angry when we leave the house late!"

Learning the differences between conflict and violence, and conflict and anger, is extremely important in the effort to build peace, in the family, within nations, and between nations. Wars erupt from conflicts, but **a conflict is not war.** Friendships survive conflict; were this not true, few if any of us would have long-time friends. Family members can strongly disagree, about many very important areas of life, without losing their love for one another. Conflict is OK. The most efficient responses to conflict and anger are nonviolent.

4 When Answered With Violence, Violence Always Escalates

Violence is inefficient, ineffective, and, when answered with violence, always escalates. In 1939 James Thurber published *The Last Flower: A Parable in Pictures*. The Film Board of Canada produced "Neighbors," an animated film based on Thurber's parable. In it, two men live next to each other. As they sit in adjoining yards reading and communicating in a friendly way, a little flower suddenly sprouts and grows right on the property line. They both notice and walk over to stoop down and smell the flower. Immediately they become competitive, pushing each other away. Each claims the flower. One builds a fence showing it on his side; the other moves the fence. They rip out the fence posts and come to blows as the flower is trampled. Their faces distort, as raging monsters, and the battle continues as they destroy each other's houses. Finally they kill each other.

Thurber's story illustrates a characteristic of violence that we must understand if we are to treat the problem. Think how we tend to feel when someone offends us, verbally abuses us, or hits us. Don't we want to hit back, only harder? We immediately get defensive and feel a need to retaliate. This impulse contributes to the main characteristic of violence: when answered with violence, it always escalates.

Violence always grows if it is answered with violence. Accepting this simple axiom, we can derive several strategies. First, when any tension erupts, it is best addressed as soon as possible, before it gets worse. The time to arrest violent behavior is as soon as it begins.

If we also understand thoroughly that violence is whatever hurts people or diminishes life, and then apply the law of escalation, we see that simple teasing (hurtful) can lead to a fist fight, then a shooting battle and death. An arms race can escalate into a war. If we don't want the big problems, we'd better treat the little ones.

If we are going to treat any problem, however, we need to know what causes it. It is easier to control symptoms, but unless we truly address the causes of violence we can treat symptoms perpetually. So what really causes violence?

5 Find the Root Cause

Many of us think violence, at least physical violence, is committed by thoughtless, hurtful, bad people. Are "bad people" the cause of violence? Is that the whole story? What causes people to do bad things? Does it just happen that some people are bad, while others are good? What, if anything, makes the difference? Is it pure chance?

In his book *The Quality School*, William Glasser lists five basic human needs: physical survival, love, power, freedom, and fun. Not everyone has all these needs fulfilled. According to our definition of violence–we define violence as anything that hurts–denial of one or more of those needs causes hurt. Therefore, that denial is violent.

Looking pro-actively, consider that in addition to physical survival, everyone you know, everyone you meet, needs love, power, freedom and fun somewhere in their lives. Keeping that idea in mind, you may be able to create new ways to interact with "difficult" people in your life.

Have you ever been denied a human need? Have you lost a job on which your survival depended? The love of someone whose love you cherished? The power to reach your goal? How did you feel? Were you angry? Frustrated? Did you want to retaliate in some way? Could that lead to your being violent?

The *Alternatives to Violence* course workbook offers a diagnostic tool we call the *Alvarez Diamond* that can be useful in analyzing human needs.

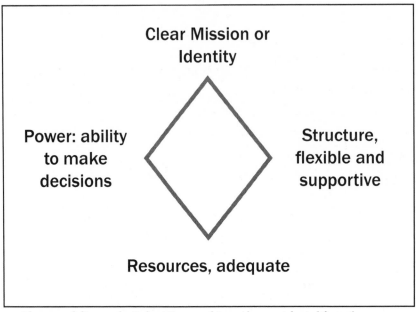

Theory and diagram by Robert Terry and Jean Alvarez. Adapted from the *Alternatives to Violence Workbook*. Akron, OH: Peace Grows, Inc. 1995.

The four points of the Alvarez Diamond represent elements that need to be balanced in a fully-functioning individual, group, community, organization, or nation. At the center top is "**mission**," or a clear purpose. Nations, companies, or groups with unclear missions can be diverted into status maintenance machines for their leaders. **Well-stated missions are often lofty, and usually not fully achieved, but they point the way forward, as would a light held before travelers in the dark.**

In individual terms, "**Identity**" is comparable to mission, and necessary for each of us. Much of the turmoil of the teenage years, for example, stems from an effort to achieve identity separate from families and peers. Marriages where individual identity is not recognized and respected can end in divorce.

On the right of the Alvarez Diamond is "**Structure**": for the individual, structure is usually provided by the family. Countless problems can arise from lack of structure. For nations, structure is the constitution. For churches, organizations, and companies, structure is found in the by-laws or organizational chart clearly outlining those responsible for various kinds of decision-making. **Structures** of all kinds need to be both **flexible** and **supportive**.

At the bottom of the Alvarez Diamond are "**Resources**," which include physical resources like food, shelter, water, and the means to obtain them, but also intellectual and spiritual resources. Think of the lottery winners who fell into bankruptcy because an abundance of resources were not balanced with mission and structure.

Often the "resources" missing can boil down to information, as when a dictator does not know facts about people being oppressed. Persons sheltered over a lifetime by extreme privilege, for example, may actually come to believe that they truly are superior beings, that the privileged and the oppressed are not the same species. Shakespeare offers a corrective to this syndrome in both *King Lear* and *The Merchant of Venice*: Shylock asks the anti-Semitic Christian court, "Hath not a Jew eyes?....If you prick him, does he not bleed?" The old monarch Lear, outdoors in a heavy storm, exclaims, "Take physic, pomp! Expose thyself to feel what wretches feel, that thou mayst shake the superflux to them and show the Heavens more just!" Lear sees a naked madman and identifies with him, then exclaims, "Is man no more than this? Consider him well. ...Unaccommodated man is no more but such a poor, bare, forked animal as thou art."

Finally, on the left of the Alvarez Diamond is "**Power,**" which here is *not* the ability, as commonly understood, to push around huge groups of other people. Power is *the ability to make decisions about one's own life*. For a nation, power is political and economic freedom. For a young person, power is the ability to choose and pursue a goal. For an elderly person, power is the ability to choose where and how to live.

Like an MRI, a thermometer or a stethoscope, the Alvarez Diamond is simply a diagnostic tool. To "read" the diamond, consider the nation, group, or person, and **consider whether or not Mission, Structure, Resources, and Power are in balance**. If they are not, what is weak or missing can illuminate the causes of problems that lead to violence and point the way toward possible solutions. These four elements need to be in balance to work most efficiently.

The fully-functioning individual who has most all their basic needs met is far less apt to be violent, at least on a personal, one-on-one sense. That they may be benefiting from an economic or social system and may be part of that system which hurts other people is another matter.

6 "The Third Way": Focus on the Perpetrator

How do you usually handle conflict? If someone insults you, do you look for "payback"? Have you thought of a "smart comeback" after the fact, and felt sad that you didn't say it right away? Have you ever simply turned away from harassment? Did you put yourself down for turning away? American TV is awash in insult exchanges–cheap substitutes for plot and character in sitcoms, and for research in news. Young people must be forgiven for thinking that insult-invention and hostile retaliation is a sign of intelligence.

An old saw holds that in confrontations, people share with animals two basic instincts: fight or flight. Fight back or you're a wimp! **Nonviolence offers a path for responding to conflict that is far more powerful than either fighting back or running away.**

"The third way" is to focus attention on the insulting or threatening person's problem. If we define violence very broadly, as anything that hurts, and we realize that violence arises from unmet human needs, it follows that people who insult others (with even mildly violent speech) have unmet needs. **Instead of flinching, fighting, or running, it's very empowering to calmly study what the attacker's needs are and try to address them.**

One of the most useful applications of this process can be practiced at home if you have teenagers. Teens often express hostility to those they really love, in order to differentiate themselves from the family and learn who they are as individuals. Into your home stalks a surly teenager: try to correct and control this person at your peril, or try to understand and address their gripe of the day. Quietly be ready to listen, and do so responsively.

No teenagers at home? Next time you come across someone who is merely grumpy, silently try to imagine their unmet needs. A clerk in a store, for example, resents being underpaid, or is very tired, bored, or ill. Instead of grumping back, imagine the possible causes and what you might say or do to salve his pain, even slightly. You may just smile and say "How are you doing?" or "Thanks," sincerely. Your kindness won't cure the underlying problem, but it can change the emotional direction of the other participant during that one small scene in life's drama.

The magic in this process is that you have armored yourself against becoming defensive and retaliating by putting your imagination and investigative skills to work. It's also fun, and clean safe intellectual exercise. You're likely to enjoy doing it and smile, which won't hurt and may help.

If you practice this third way in simple situations with people you don't know, it can become such a habit that you may be able to defuse very serious problems with people you know and care about—your own teenagers, for example, or elderly parents, or your spouse or boss. You are likely to feel empowered each time you practice. **Nonviolence is proactive. Practicing nonviolence is not only much safer than fighting back or running, it can also boost your own confidence and health.**

7 Listen

Listening actively is the major skill in the practice of nonviolence. Listening can be violent or nonviolent, and much of what passes for listening in our public life is quite violent. Asking questions then cutting off the answers, constantly and rudely interrupting others may pass for intelligent analysis, but only on TV. A measure of the endemic violence of our culture is that a few high schools have mimicked a common combative TV format.

Here is how to listen violently:

- Interrupt the speaker. Your ideas are more important, of course.

- Think about your response instead of what the speaker is saying.

- Watch other listeners in the audience instead of the speaker, or judge the speaker's choice of outfits for that day, or plan your next lunch date.

- Don't respond at all, or if you do, either point out the errors you notice in the speaker's presentation, or forcefully bring up a completely different topic.

- Do whatever you can to show your superior knowledge and grasp of the topic.

Nonviolent listening, in contrast, is done by people who are already sure of their own worth, so they don't have to prove it in constant combat. Such people:

- Listen carefully because they have genuine curiosity, the base for all learning.

- Focus intensely on what the speaker is saying.

- Never interrupt.

- Maintain eye contact with the speaker.

- Ask questions when they don't understand, and double-check by repeating back to the speaker what they do understand.

- Never insult a speaker, but if the speaker's ideas do not seem reasonable, ask for clarification.

If you disagree strongly with a speaker, say so politely, but also look for areas of concord and points of agreement. The recent resurgence of old-fashioned live storytelling, in festivals and schools, gives hope for the future of public discourse. A good storyteller, in real life, commands attentive listeners and gives them experience in nonviolent listening.

Listening is the *sine qua non*, the skill beyond compare as we seek to grow peace.

8 Turn Anger to Energy

Since the mid-1970s, assertiveness training and anger management classes have been offered by many school systems and health districts in the United States to those who have suffered or inflicted abuse. Most of us need the basic communication skills such courses offer. *Alternatives to Violence* classes review the basics of assertiveness training. Assertive behavior is honest, healthy, efficient, and nonviolent.

Again, it is helpful to remember these definitions::

- **Conflict** is a natural and normal part of life, necessary for growth.

- **Anger** is a good, natural, normal human emotion. Anger can give us energy to bring about needed change.

- **Violence** is a common but useless response to anger and conflict.

Nonviolence training offers countless ways to handle anger and manage conflict without violence. The solutions are countless because you create responses based on the specifics of your particular situation, and most situations can be dealt with nonviolently in several ways.

When we are attacked, as persons or as a nation, it is very difficult to maintain "cool" and stop the urge to hit back. Like listening, however, controlling and using the energy from anger is a skill you can practice and grow. **Nonviolence processes anger to create peaceful change: anger produces emotional energy that can be tamed and directed efficiently.** The Montgomery Bus Boycott of 1955 is one of many large-scale examples of creatively directed anger in American history.

Remember also, Axiom # 1: **Violence always escalates if it's answered with violence.** It follows that if we respond with violence to an attack, hitting back verbally or physically, the attacker's next response is likely to be still worse–more violent, more destructive. Simply absorbing the attack (non-assertively "stuffing" feelings) is *not* the answer, however.

In our endemically violent, "macho," strength-worshipping culture, admitting to feelings of pain or hurt is often considered "whining," wimpy or weak. Many of us refuse to acknowledge our own pains, fears, and hurts. When we "stuff" or repress our feelings, however, we are doing violence to ourselves, and that violence, too, can escalate and appear later, unexpected and uncontrolled.

Admitting pain, and "owning" angry feelings, is a sign of strength if it's done nonviolently. Naming the pain and calmly describing its source are the first steps in getting rid of it. Assertiveness theory asks us to make a habit of honestly stating our negative feelings, using "I-statements." Such statements help us avoid the "You did. . . " and "You always…." expressions that make others feel the need to defend themselves. Focus on the problem, not the person.

Some examples: "I feel sad when I hear obscene language." "I feel upset when socks don't get put in the laundry hamper because it gives me more work to do."   "I feel angry when I hear racist remarks because I remember Emmett Till."

Below is a simple "I-statement" chart to help organize honest responses to people whose actions leave you hurt or angry.

I feel _____
                                   (name emotion)

when _____
              ، (name negative or unwanted behavior or statement)

because _____
                              (describe negative outcome)

Emotional and psychological "strength-training" in nonviolence entails looking at attackers with respect and equanimity. Clearly state your own feelings without judging the attacker or "hitting back." Using the chart above, and the "Differences Between Violence and Nonviolence" chart in Chapter 1 as guidelines, see what happens when you role-play this process with a friend.

Practice

I feel _____
(name emotion)

when _____

_____
(name negative or unwanted behavior or statement)

because _____

_____
(describe negative outcome)

I feel _____
(name emotion)

when _____

_____
(name negative or unwanted behavior or statement)

because _____

_____
(describe negative outcome)

9   Learn Not to Flinch

Each of us has "made someone mad" at some time. In neighborhoods, it's a barking dog or a cat that's eaten the petunias, or dirty sidewalks, or garbage left on the street. In schools, it's poor grades, or inadequate playing time in the big game; in cities, code enforcement. In families, it's forgetting a thank-you note or overspending or clothes left to wrinkle in the dryer or the classic teenager's messy bedroom. So someone's mad at you. What about it?

Depending on the severity of the problem, ignoring others' anger directed at you may be the best course of action. But that's rare. Since nonviolence works so well, and is far easier than worrying or dealing with escalation and complications, it's a good idea to try a nonviolent approach. Remember, **nonviolence is active, *not* passive, but proactive**.

When you learn of their anger, or as soon as possible after you learn of it, go to the offended party and calmly ask why. For example, say in a calm, quiet tone, "I understand that you're upset with me." The simple fact that you have approached them proves that you have concern and respect for their feelings. Treated respectfully, most people will return the favor. Most people are relieved at the opportunity to rid themselves of anger, to vent and expand on its causes.

From here on, your job is active, nonviolent, responsive listening. Don't "push back" aggressively, but don't "stuff" your own feelings non-assertively either. Acknowledge the right of the offended person to have negative feelings. If you feel yourself getting angry, remember the I-statement chart. **Aim to solve the problem by focusing on the problem, not the person.** Look for common ground, something to agree on, even if you can't agree on the main point.

Practice and role-play active, nonviolent listening with someone you love.

10 Intervene Creatively

Nonviolence requires creativity. John Looney used to start this lesson by asking us to imagine walking down High Street, near The Ohio State University, and seeing a man dragging a woman by her hair down the opposite sidewalk. "What would you do?" John asked, and in those days, no one had cell phones. There are many right answers to this problem. One is, summon help from law enforcement if you can, then try to distract the offender.

Stating the obvious. One method of distraction, useful in many situations, is to *state the obvious*: Cross the street and say "You're hurting that woman." This might be called the Forrest Gump approach. In stating the obvious, you are treating the offending person with respect, and giving them the chance to respond in kind.

The offender might think you're mentally disabled, perhaps, but your presence is likely to distract him. You might also speak some gibberish or tell a long urgent story to keep the abuser distracted. You might offer to help him or suggest something even more ridiculous.

You might also be hurt by the offender. Nonviolence takes courage as well as creativity. Do not put yourself in harm's way unnecessarily. Call the police on your cell phone.

Intervention in child abuse at the supermarket: Many of us have seen parents abuse their children in public places, particularly in large stores, either verbally or physically. Laws now protect children from physical abuse that once was acceptable, but verbal and psychological abuse of children, sadly, is still plentiful in American society. The nonviolent intervener must be very careful not to make the situation worse. To avoid that, keep in mind the basic principle that violence arises from unmet human needs.

Focus your attention on what may be the unmet needs of the perpetrator. No cold disapproving stares, threats, scorn or indignation, all of which exacerbate. Instead, remember that parents and caregivers who abuse children have themselves probably been abused. You can't change their history, but you may be able to give an ounce–or even a microgram–of cure. If you can think creatively in the moment of a way to salve the pain of the abusing parent, even in the most miniscule way, you are helping the child.

Each case is different, but most of us can find a way *to show respect and care for the stressed parent.* Even the smallest gesture, for example, a smile, can help break the stress/abuse cycle. Expressing kindred feeling–for example, "I remember when mine were that age"–may prompt the stressed parent to share his or her frustration verbally with you instead of taking it out on the child.

It's extremely difficult, especially for single parents, not to have adults to talk to. In the grocery store, the park, the streets of your neighborhood, or at work, you can serve the best interests of children and society simply by being open and willing to hold a conversation with a stressed parent. Even if the conversation is just about the weather.

There are situations where the abuse is so severe that law enforcement should be notified.

Fights after school: Scores, or unresolved conflicts, that brew inside schools are often settled outside, on the way home. Anyone who lives near an urban school is likely to have witnessed fist fights or worse. Proactive nonviolence requires that adults intervene as if the fighting children were their own. When a stranger assumes a role of authority in such cases, the fighters are often shocked into peace.

Notifying school officials and law enforcement may also be appropriate. Every student should feel comfortable talking to at least one adult authority figure in their school, and ideally, such figures would all be practitioners of nonviolence.

Fights in the family: The most difficult interventions may be at home. When parents or siblings are embattled, sometimes over long periods of time, it's useful to consider the unmet needs of the participants. Feelings of being unloved or inadequately loved and respected can develop over years, and unknown to other family members. State the obvious. Listen responsively and make your own feelings, observations, and needs clear. Your example may prompt others to follow suit and clear the air.

If people are willing to talk, listening responsively works very well in almost all situations. **Listening is the primary, essential skill in nonviolence.**

11 Think Fast, Stay Calm

"It was an absolutely best-case scenario…a complete opposite of what you expected to happen. We were prepared for the worst and got the best," said Darren Moloney, a police officer in Gwinnett County, Georgia. Officer Moloney was describing a hostage's nonviolent response to a man who had just murdered four people in March 2005. Instead of fighting back, Ashley Smith let her love for her daughter dominate her actions: "I saw her face in my head almost the entire time," Smith said. **Ashley apparently conquered fear by focusing on her love for her child, and without fear, she was able to act with great intelligence.**

If you have been physically assaulted and can recall your feelings, your strongest emotion was probably fear. **Nonviolence training reduces fear—ideally, fear is erased. Freed from the grip of fear, you can think clearly, and that gives you power. You can create solutions tailored to fit the situation when your mind works at or near top efficiency.**

Americans were amazed when Ashley Smith described how she shared an inspirational book with the murderer, as well as the Bible, and told him about her beliefs and her family. Smith's husband had died in her arms after being stabbed four years earlier. She appealed to her captor's better nature, saying that if she died, her daughter would be an orphan. To calm and comfort the fleeing murderer, she gave him hope that he might be able to help others when he went to prison. After Smith made him a breakfast of pancakes with real butter–the real butter impressed him greatly–the murderer allowed her to leave to see her daughter, then he surrendered peacefully to the authorities.

When you're threatened or assaulted, it may seem impossible not to fight back or try to escape. With training and practice, however, nonviolent responses can come more easily. Since law enforcement officers are required to deal nonviolently with all assaults unless they are deadly, they are trained intensely to keep many kinds of assault from escalating to the lethal level. Law enforcement personnel in some cities have had *Alternatives to Violence* classes in addition to their regular training. Just as divider barriers on highways help prevent head-on crashes, training and practice in nonviolent self-defense can be a major lifesaver.

Nonviolence depends on mental resources and creativity, so thousands of "disarming" tactics are possible. Surprise is a powerful element in nonviolent self-defense. Unexpected responses confuse would-be attackers and change the direction of an interaction. Dorothy T. Samuel describes the astonishing response of an older woman carrying heavy groceries in a high-crime neighborhood. She heard muggers coming from behind, so just before two would-be robbers touched her, the woman turned, handed them her packages, and thanked them for helping her. The astonished boys carried the bags and walked her home safely![4] Assailants generally expect their "victims" to be fearful, and can be taken aback when people aren't afraid.

---

4   *Safe Passage on City Streets*, Nashville: Abingdon Press, 1975.

Dorothy Samuel also recounted how Jane Addams, founder of Hull House in Chicago, surprised an armed intruder who awakened her in the night. When Addams asked, "What is the trouble?" he replied that he was out of work and needed money. Addams replied, "I have no money, but if you come around in the morning I'll try to find a job for you." He left, came back the next morning, and she found him a job.[5] Addams' mind was prepared: she had recently bought Hull House, an old mansion, to serve the poor, so she already understood and sympathized with the intruder's desperation. Her concern for the attacker was clearly disarming.

Nonviolent personal defense re-directs energy. The key is to convert negative energy coming toward you to positive energy flowing out. To keep positive outgoing energy while being attacked, it helps to create a general strategy. For example, some *Alternatives to Violence* students imagine a little demon standing on the attacker's shoulder, so they focus about how to alleviate whatever pain the make-believe demon is doling out to the assailant. Such focus prevents fear.

Of course we can only guess what another's problems are, but just **in trying to imagine the possible causes of the attacker's pain, you are automatically protecting yourself from falling into a fearful, helpless victim's role and from "hitting back," which would escalate the violence. Such a nonviolent response directs energy in a proactive, kindly manner, 180 degrees from what might be expected.** We can't always overcome fear with love, but even a little concern for a violent suffering person (all violent people are suffering)

---

5   *Safe Passage*, pp. 19-20.

allows us to maintain emotional control, stay calm–or more calm than we would otherwise be, observe carefully, and–most important–listen.

Nonviolent reactions to personal attacks can prevent injury. **There is no guarantee that nonviolence will work, but people who use nonviolent self-defense have a major survival skill in their toolkit.**

12 Reach for Blue Sky: Six-Step Problem Solving

Six-step problem solving is another nonviolent tool. A Google search yields over 3 million hits on "six-step problem solving." There are many variations.

The method illustrated on the next page was developed over 30 years by a collaborative that started in the American Friends Service Committee office in Akron, Ohio, during the Cold War. Like other nonviolent methods, it takes time, but it is also supremely efficient.

The same basic method can be used by one person working alone, if necessary, or by a very large and diverse group. It can be time-consuming, but it is far more efficient than protracted conflict.

In the *Alternatives to Violence* course at Highbank Peace Education Center, "Six-Step Problem Solving" uses two triangles, upside down, one on the other, as a mnemonic device to help people remember these steps. This "six-step" method, with or without the triangles, can work in solving extremely complicated problems. On the next page is a sketch of how the triangle mnemonic works.

Six-Step Problem Solving

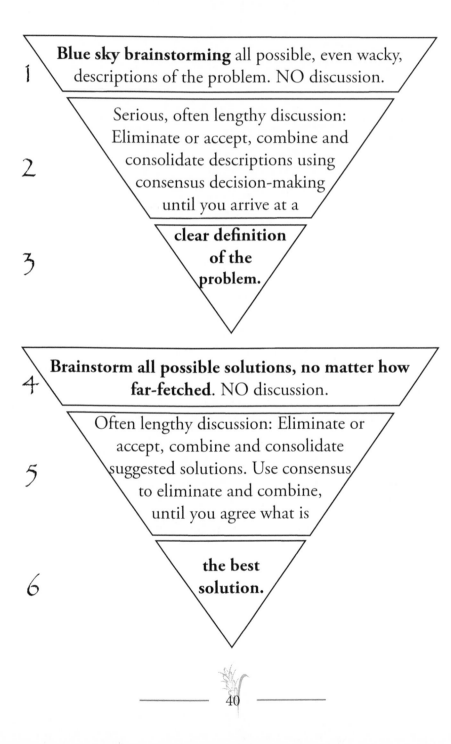

1 **Blue sky brainstorming** all possible, even wacky, descriptions of the problem. NO discussion.

2 Serious, often lengthy discussion: Eliminate or accept, combine and consolidate descriptions using consensus decision-making until you arrive at a

3 **clear definition of the problem.**

4 **Brainstorm all possible solutions, no matter how far-fetched.** NO discussion.

5 Often lengthy discussion: Eliminate or accept, combine and consolidate suggested solutions. Use consensus to eliminate and combine, until you agree what is

6 **the best solution.**

13 Grow Peace Out of Conflict: Hold a Meeting

Group meetings are the lifeblood of democracy. Slavery was abolished, women won the right to vote, schools were desegregated in the United States, and nuclear holocaust was prevented in the late 20th century—all because people held meetings. Productive meetings don't happen by chance, but there's no mystery, no high and difficult art, to having a good meeting.

The *Alternatives to Violence* course uses role-play to show how successful meetings can work. In 1979 Prill Goldthwait described two types of leadership roles—task and maintenance roles—and five common blocking roles. "Task" roles, those that keep the group moving toward a goal, are: Initiator, Information Seeker, Summarizer, and Evaluator. Maintenance roles keep relations within the group moving smoothly: Goldthwait labeled the maintenance roles Encourager, Gatekeeper, Harmonizer, and Compromiser. Blocking roles are Competer, Big Talker, Clown, Withdrawer or Drifter into Space, Self-Confessor, and Complainer.

In *Alternatives to Violence*, students "play" roles in a mock meeting. In real life, one person may fill two or more of these roles in the same meeting, as when the Initiator also becomes Self-Confessor, or the Complainer becomes the Gatekeeper. Using these labels helps build self-awareness among participants.

Before an important meeting in real life, or when a group–a school board, for example–first gather, it may be useful to write each of the labels listed below on a card, ask members to draw cards, and take ten minutes to "play" whatever role they draw. It's fun to debrief afterward, guessing each others' roles. Such a "game" will make participants aware of the difference each behavior can make. Each person contributes either positively or negatively to what's often called–as if we were helpless to change it–"group dynamics." But we can change the pattern and minimize blocking roles. We can grow peace in a violent world, starting at home and very close to home.

Task Roles

- **Initiator:** Calls the meeting, clarifies its time, place, and goal if possible.

- **Information Seeker:** Asks questions to bring out relevant facts.

- **Summarizer:** Recounts what's happened and what's been agreed to.

- **Evaluator:** Measures progress toward the group's goal.

Maintenance Roles

- **Encourager:** Helps individuals and group open up to share ideas.

- **Gatekeeper:** Makes sure everyone has a chance to participate.

- **Harmonizer:** Finds common ground among those who may be disagreeing on facts or strategies. Helps everyone relax.

- **Compromiser:** Shows how two points of view, or two strategies, can work together to achieve the goal.

Blocking Roles

- **Competer:** Napoleon has to control, besting everyone else.

- **Self-confessor:** Gives lengthy, irrelevant personal history.

- **Clown:** Uses comic talent, or effort at it, to get personal attention.

- **Complainer:** Focuses on flaws in procedure, participants, and goal.

- **Big Talker:** Doesn't listen, but talks and talks, and talks.

- **Withdrawer or Drifter into Space:** Is essentially absent from the meeting.

Nonviolent Tactics for Dealing with Blocking Roles

If you call a meeting and feel you're in Blocking City, what should you do? Respect the blockers, but be honest with them and all participants. Thank everyone for their input but remind the group about the need to finish the task at hand in a reasonable time. Suggest taking up topics that aren't germane to this meeting at another. Appoint a Gatekeeper, a Summarizer, and a Harmonizer. If time allows, play a game of assigned roles as a group before the meeting even starts: doing so may provide comic relief from tension and prevent the insidious, silent violence of wasted time.

14 Grow Peace Out of Conflict: Practice Consensus Decision-Making[6]

The word "consensus" is derived from the same root as "consent." It doesn't mean that everyone completely approves of an action or decision, but only that all parties "consent" to it. There may be differences, but the differences are not important enough for the dissenters to block passage. Instead, dissenters willingly stand aside and let the action go ahead.

Consensus is a decision-making method in which everyone involved has input to the fullest possible extent. To achieve this, the group facilitation must be nonviolent. As we have seen, there are ways through helpful and maintenance roles to provide greater assurance that everyone has a voice and that voice is heard and respected. Blocking roles tend to obstruct consensus decision-making.

Consensus isn't necessarily achieved in one meeting. Instead, it can be an ongoing process, with discussion between meetings. It's helpful if the disagreeing parties carry on communications in a less formal way outside meetings, in fact. By using the skills of active listening, clear-stating, proposing options, negotiating, and mediating, the parties at odds seek to fully understand each other. This process takes time. Feelings and perceptions, word definitions, and details

---

6   From *Alternatives to Violence Workbook*, New Edition, Akron: Peace Grows, Inc. 1995, p. 127.

about points of disagreement are clarified. Each person seeks to fully understand why the other has taken their position.

To work toward consensus, ask questions: What areas of agreement can be enlarged upon? What mutual adjustments or improved knowledge or understanding could reduce or eliminate the areas of disagreement? When progress is made toward narrowing or ending the major areas of disagreement, then consensus at the next meeting becomes more likely.

When a family selects a movie to go to, it is done by consensus. Jury verdicts are all by consensus. Whenever a group decides to do something that no one objects to, that is consensus. All Quaker business meetings have been conducted by consensus for over 350 years.

15 Grow Peace Out of Conflict: Negotiation and Mediation

We negotiate constantly: we consider the needs of others without recklessly crashing forward to fulfill our own needs and desires. You don't make noise while the baby is sleeping, you don't take all the cookies in the jar, and you don't use up the family savings account to buy a pleasure boat, all because you respect the needs of others. Negotiation is the first and most desirable of the several nonviolent conflict management methods, the next being mediation, then arbitration, and finally litigation.

Why is negotiation the most desirable method? *Because the parties themselves have full power to come to an agreement and solve their problem.* No third party is involved. The disputants are negotiating for and by themselves. Many excellent how-to books on negotiation are available, including *Getting to Yes* by Roger Fisher and William Ury. Another route to successful negotiation is to study and keep before you John Looney's "Differences Between Violence and Nonviolence" in Chapter 1 of this book.

When negotiation doesn't work–for whatever reason–people in a dispute can still proceed calmly and nonviolently, by asking for the help of a mediator. Mediation is growing in popularity across the United States. Most disputes can be settled using this highly efficient formal system of cooperative problem-solving. Mediation services are available in many cities, often at cost or free to those who can't afford to pay. In mediation, the parties still create their own agreement, but with the guidance of a third party, the professionally trained mediator. A mediator doesn't create the solution, but does steer toward one, if possible, holding the parties on course according to the rules of mediation. Formal training in mediation is available for reasonable fees in some cities, and mediation skills, like math skills, can be applied in many arenas.

16 Grow Peace Out of Conflict: Arbitration and Litigation

If mediation doesn't work, still another nonviolent method is available: arbitration. Arbitration is more expensive and time-consuming and removed from the parties themselves, but it is necessary in many kinds of disputes, particularly complicated labor-management conflicts that affect large groups of people. A highly trained (and very well paid) professional arbitrator studies the conflict with each party, often spending a great deal of time finding the facts. The arbitrator then creates the solution.

Before the process begins, the parties decide whether or not the outcome will be "binding." If so, disagreeing parties agree *in advance* to respect and follow the arbitrator's decision. If they enter "non-binding arbitration," they can wait for the arbitrator's decision and take it or leave it, but in either case, they have to pay high fees for the arbitrator's professional service.

So we see that negotiation is a great way to save money and time, and to prevent stress. Memorizing John Looney's "Differences" chart can really pay off, but even that chart points out that nonviolence takes time—not as much time as violence and war, but significant time.

A fourth nonviolent problem-solving method is litigation, or resort to the courts. This should be a last resort method. When you sue your neighbor over a barking dog, you're handing away a huge amount of personal power as well as money to other people whom you don't know. When conflicts are taken to court, as we all know if we've been in court for a trial, the disputing parties are not even allowed to talk to each other! The judge or jury, who are essentially strangers, come up with the solution to a litigated dispute. On this continuum of more and more serious methods, negotiation, mediation, arbitration and litigation, you lose more and more power to decide your own fate. Stay with negotiation if it's at all possible!

Listen. The major nonviolence skill–listening–is the major step in any negotiation, whether it's about a complicated sales or labor contract, where your family's going on vacation, or when your daughter will be home after the prom. Active, responsive listening is crucial.

Listen to yourself. People who "give in" to others most of the time, aka non-assertive persons, should beware of negotiating until they've taken plenty of time to list and clarify their own needs. If you are such a person, you may want to join a support group or discuss your situation with a friend or advisor. Many cities offer counseling services at no or low cost. Those of us who have been trained from early childhood to suppress anger and to be selfless, kind, giving people sometimes need help to understand that we, too, deserve space on the planet as individuals, and that our needs are as valid as anyone's, and to be respected. Often the best action we can take, for those we love and for ourselves, is to seek help from a counselor.

Ask. Don't assume or guess what other people want or need. Sometimes we are quite sure that we know what others' needs are, only to find that we were suffering under a misperception. It's best to ask and double-check. Ask clearly and openly, then allow plenty of time to listen for a full answer.

Clarify. Avoid being "violent" either to yourself or the people with whom you're negotiating. Go in knowing what your own feelings and needs are and state them as clearly as possible. **Help the other party understand exactly what you require.** In many disputes, it's simply to hear the words, "I'm sorry" from the other party. If so, say so, and everyone can proceed back to the garden!

Successful negotiation is good manners. Ink has been shed for centuries to describe "good manners," and an easy, practical, boiled-down version appears in the "Differences" chart at the beginning of this book. Reading and thinking about these principles will stand you in good stead in all areas of life, including the business world.

17 Embrace Nonviolence as a Lifestyle

Each of the world's major religions–Judaism, Christianity, Islam, Confucianism, Buddhism and Hinduism–require their faithful to behave peacefully, and they all admonish against war and violence. In the west, Jesus of Nazareth is the best known teacher of nonviolence, but **Buddha, Confucius, Moses, the Hebrew prophets before and after Moses, and Muhammad all emphasized the necessity for peaceful behavior among their followers. Native American traditions also emphasize respect for life.**

The Sixth Commandment of Moses is "Thou shalt not kill." Following in Moses' tradition, Jesus tells his disciples, "I say unto you, that ye resist not evil: but whosoever shall smite thee on thy right cheek, turn to him the other also. " In the same Abrahamic tradition, the Prophet Muhammad admonished believers: "Hurt no one so that no one can hurt you."

Culture and religion are not the same, however. Many who heard about the other cheek in Sunday school soon dropped the idea as one of several rules in the Bible that good Christians can safely ignore, because we live in an extremely violent culture. Western culture is success-oriented in a material sense, made up of "winners" and "losers." Winners can run faster, hit harder, make more money. Some people even think that "winners" and "winning" in the material sense are evidence of God's reward to the "good." Conversely, material poverty is sometimes seen as evidence of failure brought on by one's own choices.

Possibly, however, American culture is changing. In the summer of 2006, the "richest" person on the planet, Bill Gates, a middle-aged American, quit his job to spend more time giving away money. The next week, the second-"richest" American, Warren Buffett, matched his friend's multi-billion dollar gift, saying that great inherited wealth would not be good for his own children. They may have re-defined the word "rich."

Mohandas K. Gandhi and Dr. Martin Luther King, Jr. made nonviolence a lifestyle, as have millions of their students and followers. The empowering traditions of nonviolence are far older and more widespread, however. Black Elk, the Oglala Sioux Native American who witnessed the battle at Little Big Horn and lived into the 20th century, generously shared his ancient culture with two European-American scholars, John Neihardt and Joseph Epes Brown.

In this statement, Black Elk represents nonviolent thinkers from many eras and cultures around the planet:

The first peace, which is the most important, is that which comes within the souls of people when they realize their relationship, their oneness, with the universe and all its powers, and when they realize that at the center of the universe dwells the Great Spirit, and that its center is really everywhere, it is within each of us. This is the real Peace, and the others are but reflections of this. The second peace is that which is made between two individuals and the third is that which is made between two nations. But above all you should understand that there can never be peace between nations until there is known that true peace, which, as I have often said, is within the souls of people.[7]

---

7   *The Sacred Pipe: Black Elk's Account of the Seven Rites of the Oglala Sioux.* Recorded and Edited by Joseph Epes Brown. Norman and London: University of Oklahoma Press, 1953, p. 115.

About the Authors

John Townsend Looney (1916-2005) pioneered development of a comprehensive conflict resolution course entitled Alternatives to Violence in the early 1970s. Looney's colleague Danene Bender and several John Looney Memorial Interns at the Northeast Ohio American Friends Service Committee have published the *Alternatives to Violence* course on the Internet. Readers of this book are encouraged to visit **alternativestoviolencecourse.org** for more information.

Kezia Vanmeter Sproat opened Highbank Farm Peace Education Center in Chillicothe, Ohio, in 1994. The Center hosts advanced *Alternatives to Violence* courses and creates educational materials. In 2002, Dr. Sproat was honored by Morehouse College for her response to 9/11, "A Short Course in Nonviolence," which condensed Looney's basic lessons to 271 words. *A Short Course* is available for free download at:

http://**BeginningNonviolence.blogspot.com**

55252205R00044

Made in the USA
Charleston, SC
24 April 2016

movement in schools, churches, and colleges may prevent some of the endemic bullying in many areas of American culture, perhaps most notably in mass communications and in schools.

We can heal the fear-based interactions that lead to violence. If we know and look for practical alternatives to violence, and honor and celebrate them in everyday life, we too are likely to understand, as John did, that nonviolence is far more efficient than violence in addressing human problems. Nonviolence is, in the words of Richard Gregg, "moral jiu-jitsu," a way to re-direct and maximize energy.[2]

The *Alternatives to Violence* course emphasizes that the same basic nonviolence skills can be applied on the personal, family, community, national, and international levels. In this book, I have omitted the national defense sections because the subject is now well-covered elsewhere. In this book, we focus on personal action.

Nonviolence is powerful but not necessarily easy. Most humans already have many nonviolence skills, but we need to shine them up. If we redirect our minds away from revenge and go confidently in nonviolence toward a more open life, we too can sow peace and grow still more peace.

Kezia Vanmeter Sproat

Highbank Farm Peace Education Center
Chillicothe, Ohio

---

2   Richard Gregg, *The Power of Nonviolence.* New York: Schocken Books, 1959.

The *Alternatives to Violence* course is designed to teach the principles, skills, strategies and techniques of nonviolence. Teachers and students work interactively. They role-play conflict situations and create ways to apply nonviolence theory to many types of common problems.

At his passing in 2005, John was working on a "how to" book for the general public that followed the general structure of the *Alternatives to Violence* course manual. John outlined this book and drafted four chapters. His widow Adele asked me to complete it. *Beginning Nonviolence* is not a substitute for the *Alternatives to Violence* course, but an introduction. As John often pointed out, each of the course sessions could be a life's work; indeed, his nickname for the course was "Nonviolence 101." Like many other worthy human endeavors, nonviolence is a lifetime study, never perfected but highly rewarding in the pursuit.

Interaction with other people, preferably those with very different backgrounds and experience, is crucial to developing skill and confidence in creating and applying nonviolent strategies. For that reason, the exercises in this book are designed for groups. Working together, we discover each other, drop our fears of difference, and build confidence and trust. We cannot effectively teach the *Alternatives to Violence* course to people whom we cannot literally see and hear and touch.

So why offer a book? Our immediate and practical purpose is to show readers that both a broad and a particular peace is not the stuff of remote dreams. John analyzed and identified ways to find viable, practical "how-to" *alternatives* to violence. A resurgence of the *Alternatives to Violence*

stand-down came after John and thousands of other peace activists here and in Europe worked toward it for nearly 40 years, John himself having personally organized 200 groups for Ohio Nuclear Freeze.

In 1970, when John looked for instructional materials on peacemaking, he found Fran Schmidt's books for children,[1] but none for adults. He worked with The Society of Friends and several northeastern Ohio churches to develop and test a nonviolence training course for adults called *Alternatives to Violence*. The result of team effort over several years, the first *Alternatives to Violence Workbook: A Manual for Teaching Peacemaking to Youth and Adults* compiled by John, Prill Goldthwait, and Kathy Bickmore, was published in 1984. In 1985, John and Danene Bender started a new nonprofit in Akron, Peace GROWS, Inc., to support and promulgate the course. An expanded new edition of the *Alternatives to Violence Workbook* followed in 1986.

John spent the last twenty years of his life using the course to "spread nonviolence" as far as possible. After his death, his colleague Danene Bender funded a Memorial Internship in John's name at the Northeast Ohio Office of the American Friends Service Committee. Danene and the five John Looney Memorial Interns she has mentored have created the website alternativestoviolencecourse.org. The complete course is thus available free of charge worldwide. The website also enables users to form groups to study the course together.

---

1   Fran Schmidt and her sister Grace Contrino Abrams wrote *Creative Conflict Solving for Kids,* and after Grace's passing Fran founded the Grace Contrino Abrams Peace Education Foundation, for which she wrote very popular materials for teaching children peaceful problem solving. The Grace Contrino Abrams Foundation was re-named the Peace Education Foundation. A description of Fran's methods may be found in Marjorie K. Hanson. *A Conflict Resolution/Student Mediation Program: Effects on Student Attitudes and Behaviors. ERS Spectrum Journal of School Research and Information,* Fall 1994, Vol. 12, No. 4.

Preface

More than one sophisticate has asserted that "there will always be wars." During the mid-20ᵗʰ century build-up of nuclear weapons in the United States and Russia, we learned that if there was another war, there would be no "always," but nuclear night.

To assert that peace is impossible in any human society is a common pseudo-intellectual error. Understanding that peace is possible is the logical and practical first step in peace-building. Conversion from violence to nonviolence for our culture and for us as individuals is a long process, but we can learn it. It is not easy, but the world is learning it.

John Townsend Looney (1916-2005) told those of us who were privileged to be his students that after Dr. Martin Luther King, Jr. was killed in 1968, he was amazed that Dr. King's methods were not being taught in the schools. Because Dr. King's nonviolent methods obviously worked, John thought everyone should be trained to use what we now call Ghandian-Kingian nonviolence, and not just in crisis, but at work, at home, every day.

As John did all his adult life, if we study and work toward peace, we will get there: John himself worked toward and lived to see the disintegration of the greatest threat ever to face humanity and the earth. The American-Soviet nuclear

Table of Contents